Mary,
For a very special friend
who has brightened some sad
days, eased the burden of
some hard days, and has
shown me and shared with
me the true gift of friendship

Your friend always,
Linda
June '92

Text copyright © MCMXCI Fay Angus
Illustration copyright © MCMXCI The C.R. Gibson Company
No part of this book may be reproduced by any means without written
permission of the publisher.
Published by The C.R. Gibson Company
All rights reserved
ISBN 0-8378-2064-2
GB628

The Gentle Art Of Being There

Fay Angus

Illustrated by Anne Portenstein Hope

The C.R. Gibson Company, Norwalk, Connecticut 06856

This is a celebration of the gift of friendship and the blessed feelings of just knowing that you, my friend, are there in my heart. From my heart to yours...

FAY ANGUS

The Blessing of Friendship

The heartbeat of
love and friendship,

The pulse of the
hearth and the home,

is someone there,
to care and to share,
someone to call our own.

Oh the comfort, the inexpressible comfort of feeling safe with a person; having neither to weigh thoughts nor measure words but to pour them all out, just as it is, chaff and grain together, knowing that a faithful hand will take and sift them, keeping what is worth keeping, and then, with the breath of kindness blow the rest away.

GEORGE ELIOT

So sweet a gift in friendship is the gift of availability. The blessed comfort of knowing there is someone we can depend upon.

The crown of these is made of love and friendship, and sits high upon the forehead of humanity.
JOHN KEATS

A friend is someone who is there to meet us exactly where we're at, to accept us for who we are and to encourage us to grow into all we can become.

Every great glorious once in awhile our lives are touched, uplifted and enriched by those friends who, like ministering angels, bring to us that ultimate gift...the gift of themselves. The gentle art of being there!

Friends Are...

LIFE ENHANCERS—
pearls of great price
who with their soft and
radiant glow
give us quiet strength
in the midst of turmoil,
grace in the time of trial
and gladness in the sheer comfort
of their presence.

PATH SOFTENERS—
tender hearts
who by the dearness of
gentle words
and acts of loving kindness
are consistently there for us. . .
who instinctively know what to do
and how to do it
to make our daily walk
so much easier.

KINDRED SPIRITS—
mirror images of our inner selves,
who dream our dreams,
share our secret longings,
understand our frailties
and keep alive the wonder
of all we are
and all we'd like to be.

Thank You For Being You

For taking time
to make time
to listen to my heart,

for bringing out the
best in me
together or apart,

for side-by-side
companionship
with cheery words and smile,

for walking through
the tiring pace
of that extra mile. . .

for the firm grip
of steady hands
on many a slippery day,

for holding me
in the arms of faith
and teaching me to pray,

for all that's good
and all that's true
for all that is uniquely you,

I'm giving blessed thanks!

In Praise

I'm praising God for you today,
the things you do,
the things you say.
Any time of the day or night,
pouring rain or sunshine bright,
you're always there for me!

You Brighten My Days

Fragile times
on a less than perfect day,

storm clouds
gathering in my heart . . .

You came
with one red rose
in a slender golden box.

Sitting here beside me,
you listened to my silence.

The day you called,
oh happy day,
the sun rose in my heart
and chased the darkness
of my fears away!

A friend is someone who is there when you need them, and still there when you don't.

A friend is someone who will take your hand in theirs and say, "I believe in you!"

Friends are the guardians of each other's hearts and they exchange the keys of trust.

If gratitude were gold your storehouse would be full, because with each loving act of kindness I'd return in coin to you.

Wonder

How wondrously
blessed I will always be,
that the likes of you
likes the likes of me!

Propped against the pillows
with a late night cup of tea,
I'm thinking of you
and wondering. . .
by any chance are you awake,
thinking too, of me?

Uniquely You and Me

My friends are like a flock of birds
each of a different feather,
some flying high against the sky
strong—in all sorts of weather.

Some like a little hummingbird
hovering in place,
or darting quickly here and there
with beauty and with grace.

One is a golden song bird
with a lovely voice,
God composed a special song,
she was His special choice.

Some are perky chickadees
who flutter more than fly,
they hop about from bush to bush
and are a little shy.

Jesus chose the sparrow,
unadorned and plain,
"I see the sparrow fall," He said.
He sees and knows our pain.

However strong or weak our wings,
God gave us each our own,
exactly right for who we are
to take us safely home.

Sorrow like a stream loses itself in many channels—while joy, like a ray of the sun, reflects with great ardor and quickness when it rebounds from the heart of a friend.

ANONYMOUS

Trustworthy and True

"Who is a friend like me?" said the shadow to the body. "I am with you in the sunlight, I am with you in the moonlight, who is as good a friend as me?"

"Ah, yes indeed," said the body to the shadow. "You are with me in the sunlight, you are with me in the moonlight, but. . .where are you when neither sun nor moon is shining? Where are you in the darkness?" A friend is there to walk with us through the darkness. Albert Schweitzer said that when we walk together in the darkness the light we have within ourselves shines forth to brighten

up the path. We can get to know each other
"without needing to pass our hands over each
other's faces, or to intrude in each other's hearts."
My friend does not need a why or wherefore. My
friend is simply there.

It is when we are alone that we are the least alone.

ST. AUGUSTINE

Someone There

Someone is there beside you
to take your hand and guide you,
Someone is always with you,
every moment, night or day.

He knows your joy and sorrow
through today and each tomorrow,
His presence, wrapped around you,
He is just a prayer away.

When you think you've no one with you,
when you're frightened and alone,
listen carefully for His whisper,
"I've made your heart My home!"

A Prayer for You

You said a prayer
for me today
I felt it
like a rush
of angel wings
swirling 'round about
to catch me up
and lift me to
new heights of hope.

You said a prayer
for me today
and filled the
darkness of my night
with dancing stars.

You said a prayer
for me today
and peace fell
like a mantle
on my cold
and clammy heart—
to wrap it
in a quiet strength.

And now. . .
restored,
renewed. . .
dear gentle friend,
I'm on my knees
to say a prayer
a special prayer
for you.

From quiet homes and first beginning,
Out to the undiscovered ends,
There's nothing worth the wear of winning,
But laughter and the love of friends.

HILAIRE BELLOC

*I try to make the light in other people's eyes my
sun, the music in other's ears my symphony, the
smile of other's lips my happiness.*

HELEN KELLER

*Life is to be fortified by many friendships. To love,
and to be loved, is the great happiness of existence.*

SYDNEY SMITH

Memories of You

Star-kissed nights,
cheer filled days,
happy thoughts
along the way.

A beacon of faith
and guiding light,
love always love
shining bright.

Your lighted window
at journey's end,
the caring heart of
a cherished friend.

A song to share
and a friendly smile. . .
these are blessings
that make life worthwhile.

Friends Forever

We'll not say goodbye,
not ever, dear friend,
we'll just say cheerio!
Though our roads may fork
and our pathways bend,
I want you always to know. . .

We are knit together
with a golden cord
of a friendship tested and true.
Across many miles
and the passing years,
I'm here waiting and watching for you!

Deep within the heart of me
in a special place,
I have a hidden treasure—
it's the memory of you.